CHRISTIAN CLASSICS

CLASSICS

TERESA OF ÁVILA

Inner Joy

6 studies
for individuals
or groups
with study notes

Dale & Sandy Larsen

CAROLYN NYSTROM, Series Editor

InterVarsity Press
Downers Grove, Illinois

InterVarsity Press
P.O. Box 1400, Downers Grove, IL 60515-1426
World Wide Web: www.ivpress.com
E-mail: mail@ivpress.com

*InterVarsity Press® is the book-publishing division of InterVarsity Christian Fellowship/USA®,
a student movement active on campus at hundreds of universities, colleges and schools of
nursing in the United States of America, and a member movement of the International
Fellowship of Evangelical Students. For information about local and regional activities, write
Public Relations Dept., InterVarsity Christian Fellowship/USA, 6400 Schroeder Rd., P.O. Box
7895, Madison, WI 53707-7895, or visit the IVCF website at <www.ivcf.org>.*

All Scripture quotations, unless otherwise indicated, are taken from the Holy Bible, New
International Version®. NIV®. *Copyright ©1973, 1978, 1984 by International Bible Society.
Used by permission of Zondervan Publishing House. All rights reserved.*

Excerpts from the Complete Works of Teresa of Ávila *reprinted by permission of Sheed and
Ward, an Apostolate of the Priests of the Sacred Heart, 7373 S. Lovers Lane Rd., Franklin, WI
53132.*

Cover and interior illustrations: Roberta Polfus

ISBN 0-8308-2083-3

Printed in the United States of America ∞

P	18	17	16	15	14	13	12	11	10	9	8	7	6	5	4	3	2	1
Y	16	15	14	13	12	11	10	09	08	07	06	05	04	03	02			

CONTENTS

Introducing
Teresa of Ávila

"The Lord showed me the man I'm going to marry," Christine told us. The two hadn't yet formally met, but she was sure God had spoken to her. Unfortunately the young man must not have received the same message because within a few months the Lord told Christine she was going to marry somebody else.

Christine got her guidance from inner promptings that she interpreted as the voice of God. While certainly God can lead that way—and he definitely has led us that way on occasion—we have learned to be skeptical of believers who receive most of their guidance from their subjective feelings.

In particular, we shy away when someone claims a vision or revelation from God. And many times it is the people who talk the most about hearing directly from God who later crash and burn spiritually. As they depend less and less on the written Word, the teachings of the church and the counsel of friends, they drift into sin and sometimes abandon their faith entirely.

So what would we do with the job of writing a study guide based on the writings of a sixteenth-century Spanish mystic? From the little we knew about Teresa of Ávila, we expected to find her writings full of compelling but irrational passion, detached from earthly realities. She would be interesting, sure, but could she be trusted?

To our joy and relief, Teresa turned out to be delightfully down-to-earth. Digging into her writings, we did not find a hermit living in isolation in her own private relationship with God. We found an energetic woman who kept busy traveling and teaching, founding and administering convents, serving as spiritual mother to little families of younger nuns, reforming convent practice, appealing for funds and fighting the battles of church politics.

Through all this hard work, in her deepest soul Teresa still lived in a private place where she experienced God. She was constantly disappointed by her own failings and constantly amazed by his overcoming love. Her body grew increasingly frail, but her spirit burned brighter with love for her Lord.

And all along this remarkable woman was writing, producing such lengthy works that it is hard to see how she found time and energy in the midst of her other duties. If her writings are wordy and repetitive, it is because she apparently wrote off the top of her head—or more accurately out of her deepest heart.

> [Teresa's] ideas and sentiments spring spontaneously to her mind and spirit. Her pen runs freely—sometimes too freely for her mind to keep pace with it. Her memory, as she frequently confesses, is poor and her few quotations are seldom entirely accurate. But she is, without the slightest doubt, a born writer; and, when a person belonging to that rare and fortunate class knows nothing of artifice, casts aside convention, and writes as the spirit dictates, the result can never be disappointing.[1]

Teresa de Cepeda y Ahumada was born in 1515 in Ávila, Spain, the city that remained central to her life's work. She lived until 1582. Therefore, the context of her spiritual pilgrimage is Europe of the sixteenth century.

During that span of time the Catholic Church dominated the lives of most Europeans, while the Protestant Reformation was

---

[1]"General Introduction to the Works of St. Teresa," in *Complete Works of Teresa of Ávila*, trans. E. A. Peers (New York: Sheed & Ward, 1946).

growing—not only Lutherans but Calvinists, Baptists, Anglicans and other groups resisting the authority of Rome. Catholicism responded with its own internal reformation that would define and strengthen traditional church doctrine. The first Bible in Spanish appeared in 1569, over forty years after William Tyndale's New Testament in English. Teresa remained loyal to her church, yet she had the heart of a reformer, battling the worldliness that had taken over many convents.

The span of Teresa's life was also the time Europe looked west across the ocean to the New World. It was the beginning of the flood of European exploration and conquest of the Americas. Dedicated Catholic missionaries went east and west, pioneering missions in the Americas as well as Asia and Africa.

As for Teresa herself, she seemed marked for God from the beginning. She wrote in her autobiography, *Life of St. Teresa of Jesus,* "I never saw my parents inclined to anything but virtue." There were twelve children, and she considered herself her father's favorite. She was especially close to one brother near her own age:

> We used to read the lives of saints together; and, when I read of the martyrdoms suffered by saintly women for God's sake, I used to think they had purchased the fruition of God very cheaply; and I had a keen desire to die as they had done, not out of any love for God of which I was conscious, but in order to attain as quickly as possible to the fruition of the great blessings which, as I read, were laid up in Heaven. I used to discuss with this brother of mine how we could become martyrs.[2]

Teresa and her brother decided to go out among the Muslims in Spain, "begging our bread for the love of God, so that they might behead us there." The pair never carried out their plan; she reported later that "our greatest hindrance seemed to be that we had a father and a mother." So they changed their strategy:

[2]Ibid.

When I saw that it was impossible for me to go to any place where they would put me to death for God's sake, we decided to become hermits, and we used to build hermitages, as well as we could, in an orchard which we had at home. We would make heaps of small stones, but they at once fell down again, so we found no way of accomplishing our desires. But even now it gives me a feeling of devotion to remember how early God granted me what I lost by my own fault.[3]

When Teresa was twelve years old, her mother died at age thirty-three, and in her grief the young girl prayed to the Virgin Mary to be a mother to her. She relates that as she grew into womanhood, she went away from God and fell into sin. She does not go into detail about her sins. It appears they were in the category of personal vanity, craving friends' approval and wasting time. We look on such faults as nothing worse than typical adolescent immaturity, but they troubled Teresa's conscience because they were signs that she was not solely devoted to Christ.

At about age sixteen Teresa entered the Augustinian Convent of St. Mary of Grace in Ávila, not as a nun but as a boarder and student who didn't take the religious life very seriously. Her situation was a common one in Spain for young girls not yet pledged to be married. She wrote, "I remained in this convent for a year and a half, and was much the better for it. . . . By the end of my time there, I was much more reconciled to being a nun—though not in that house, because of the very virtuous practices which I had come to hear that they observed and which seemed to me altogether excessive."[4] She explains how God then intervened in her life:

At this time, though I was not careless about my own improvement, the Lord became more desirous of preparing me for the state of life which was best for me. He sent me a serious illness, which forced me to return to my father's house. When I got better, they took me to see my sister, who was living in a village. . . . On the road leading to my

---

[3]Ibid.
[4]Ibid.

sister's lived one of my father's brothers, a widower, who was a very
shrewd man and full of virtues. . . . It was his practice to read good
books in Spanish and his conversation was ordinarily about God and
the vanity of the world. He made me read to him; and, although I did
not much care for his books, I acted as though I did. . . . Though I
stayed here for only a few days, such was the impression made on
my heart by the words of God, both as read and as heard, and the
excellence of my uncle's company, that I began to understand the
truth, which I had learned as a child, that all things are nothing, and
that the world is vanity and will soon pass away. I began to fear that,
if I had died of my illness, I should have gone to hell; and though,
even then, I could not incline my will to being a nun, I saw that this
was the best and safest state, and so, little by little, I determined to
force myself to embrace it.[5]

In 1536 Teresa entered the Carmelite Convent of the Incarnation
at Ávila as a novice. She took her vows the following year. She con-
tinued to seek the Lord and deepen her life of prayer, not only
through the liturgy of the church but in her own spontaneous com-
munication with God.

Teresa's writings make it clear that she was not seeking any mys-
tical experience for its own sake. She was simply seeking closeness
with her Lord. About 1555 she began to experience what she considered God's inner voice, and she also began to have visions and
revelations. Such mysticism can be taken as a threat to religious
authority, even when it springs from love for God.

Mysticism makes the institutional church nervous because, carried
to its logical conclusion, it does away with the need for the priest-
hood and the sacraments. The mystic emphasizes personal religion
and his or her direct relationship to God. The ultimate goal of the
mystic is to lose himself or herself in the essence of God. The Christian mystic usually stresses the personal reality of Christ and seeks
personal union with God through the Son. Often this ultimate union
comes in a blinding flash of supreme ecstasy. In short, Christian

mysticism is contemplative, personal and usually practical.[6]

Teresa was no rebel against the church. She wrote of her private experiences because she was commanded to do so by her superiors, and she put high value on obedience. But she protested, "I have no learning, nor have I led a good life, nor do I get my information from a learned man or from any other person whatsoever. Only those who have commanded me to write this know that I am doing so, and at the moment they are not here. I am almost stealing the time for writing, and that with great difficulty, for it hinders me from spinning and I am living in a poor house and have numerous things to do."[7]

What are the long-term results of the time Teresa stole for writing?

She is a mystic—and more than a mystic. Her works, it is true, are well known in the cloister and have served as nourishment to many who are far advanced on the *Way of Perfection,* and who, without her aid, would still be beginners in the life of prayer. Yet they have also entered the homes of millions living in the world and have brought consolation, assurance, hope and strength to souls who, in the technical sense, know nothing of the life of contemplation.

Her works are read and re-read by Spaniards to this day and translated again and again into foreign languages. Probably no other book by a Spanish author is as widely known in Spain as the *Life* or the *Interior Castle* of St. Teresa, with the single exception of Cervantes's immortal *Don Quixote.* It is surely amazing that a woman who lived in the sixteenth century, who never studied in the Schools or pored over tomes of profound learning, still less aspired to any kind or degree of renown, should have won such a reputation, both among scholars and among the people.[8]

---

[6]Robert D. Linder, "Reform: Rome Responds," in *Eerdmans Handbook to the History of Christianity* (Grand Rapids, Mich.: Eerdmans, 1977), pp. 417-19.
[7]*Life of St. Teresa of Jesus,* in *Complete Works of Teresa of Ávila.*
[8]"General Introduction to the Works of St. Teresa."

Translation Note

We found the *Complete Works of Teresa of Ávila* on the Christian Classics Ethereal Library website and used that source to write this study guide. However, when we later returned to that site, the *Complete Works* was gone! After digging around a bit more, we were able to discover that the Peers translation we were using is no longer in public domain due to a change in copyright law. We received permission for its use here from the publisher, Sheed & Ward, who holds the copyright. However, the book is not in print.

Under further reading, we list another translator's collection, which is currently in print, a link to *The Way of Perfection* and secondary sources about Teresa's life. Hopefully, more of her work will come back into print. In the meantime we are grateful to have been able to offer you this taste of St. Teresa.

How to Use a Christian Classics Bible Study

Christian Classics Bible studies are designed to introduce some of the key writers, preachers and teachers who have shaped our Christian thought over the centuries. Each guide has an introduction to the life and thought of a particular writer and six study sessions. The studies each have an introduction to the particular themes and writings in that study and the following components.

READ ———————————————————————————
This is an excerpt from the original writings.

GROUP DISCUSSION OR PERSONAL REFLECTION ——————
These questions are designed to help you explore the themes of the reading.

INTO THE WORD ————————————————————————
This includes a key Scripture to read and explore inductively. The text picks up on the themes of the study session.

ALONG THE ROAD ————————————————————
These are ideas to carry you further and deeper into the themes of the study. Some can be used in a group session; many are for personal use and reflection.

The study notes at the end of the guide offer further helps and background on the study questions.

May these writings and studies enrich your life in Christ.

1
GET MOVING!
Hebrews 12:1-13

*A*re we there yet?" "How far is it?" "When are we gonna get there?" Nothing makes a long drive feel longer than those whining questions from young passengers in the back seat. As the miles pile up, the parents silently ask the same questions.

On spiritual journeys believers ask the Lord similar questions, maybe in more sophisticated words: "Aren't we finished with this process yet?" "How much longer is this going to take?" "When will I arrive at maturity?" We would rather skip the rough bumps, traffic jams and detours of our trek toward godliness.

Teresa of Ávila reminds us that we are going somewhere and the road is hard and dangerous. Why stroll when we can stride? Slow travel and frequent stops only make the trip more difficult. We must get going, keep going and get there. She wrote in *Interior Castle: Third Mansions*, "Our own task is only to journey with good speed so that we may see the Lord."

In 1577 Teresa's superiors commanded her to write a treatise on prayer. While considering how to approach the subject, she had a vision of the human soul as a great diamond in the shape of a castle. Within the castle in a series of layers were seven mansions and at the center was the glory of God. She describes each room through which the soul passes as it moves toward God. The "daughters" referred to in this excerpt are the nuns at the Convent of St. Joseph in Ávila, which she had founded in 1562.

 FACING THE JOURNEY ——————————————————

INTERIOR CASTLE: THIRD MANSIONS

Do you think, daughters, if we could get from one country to another in a week, it would be advisable, with all the winds and snow and floods and bad roads, to take a year over it? Would it not be better to get the journey over and done with? For there are all these obstacles for us to meet and there is also the danger of serpents. Oh, what a lot I could tell you about that! Please God I have got farther than this myself—though I often fear I have not!

When we proceed with all this caution, we find stumbling-blocks everywhere; for we are afraid of everything, and so dare not go farther, as if we could arrive at these Mansions by letting others make the journey for us! That is not possible, my sisters; so, for the love of the Lord, let us make a real effort: let us leave our reason and our fears in His hands and let us forget the weakness of our nature which is apt to cause us so much worry. Let our superiors see to the care of our bodies; that must be their concern: our own task is only to journey with good speed so that we may see the Lord. Although we get few or no comforts here, we shall be making a great mistake if we worry over our health, especially as it will not be improved by our anxiety about it—that I well know. I know, too, that our progress has nothing to do with the body, which is the thing that matters least. What the journey which I am referring to demands is great humility, and it is the lack of this, I think, if you see what I mean, which prevents us from making progress. We may think we have advanced only a few steps, and we should believe that this is so and that our sisters' progress is much more rapid; and further we should not only want them to consider us worse than anyone else, but we should contrive to make them do so.

If we act thus, this state is a most excellent one, but otherwise we shall spend our whole lives in it and suffer a thousand troubles and miseries. Without complete self-renunciation, the state is very arduous and oppressive, because, as we go along, we are laboring under the burden of our miserable nature, which is like a great load of earth and has not to be borne by those who reach the later Mansions. In these present Mansions the Lord does not fail to recompense us with just measure, and even generously, for He always gives us much more than we deserve by granting us a spiritual sweetness much greater than we can obtain from the pleasures and distractions of this life. But I do not think that He gives many consolations, except when He occasionally invites us to see what is happening in the remaining Mansions, so that we may prepare to enter them.

You will think that spiritual sweetness and consolations are one and the same thing: why, then, this difference of name? To me it seems that they differ a very great deal, though I may be wrong. . . . Once you understand the nature of each, you can strive to pursue the one which is better. This latter is a great solace to souls whom God has brought so far, while it will make those who think they have everything feel ashamed; and if they are humble they will be moved to give thanks. Should they fail to experience it, they will feel an inward discouragement—quite unnecessarily, however, for perfection consists not in consolations, but in the increase of love; on this, too, will depend our reward, as well as on the righteousness and truth which are in our actions.

 GROUP DISCUSSION OR PERSONAL REFLECTION——

1. Teresa wrote that "when we proceed with all this caution, we find stumbling-blocks everywhere." As you move forward on your own spiritual journey, where are you tempted to be overly cautious and why?

2. A lack of "great humility" is another quality that Teresa says "prevents us from making progress." How does humility contribute to our spiritual progress?

3. What do you think Teresa meant by "spiritual sweetness" and "consolations," and how might they differ?

4. Why is the increase of love far more important than receiving consolations from God?

 INTO THE WORD ⸻⸻⸻⸻⸻⸻⸻⸻⸻⸻⸻⸻⸻

5. *Read Hebrews 12:1-13.* What does the writer of this passage urge believers to do?

6. What attitudes does the writer urge believers to take on?

7. In what ways did Jesus show boldness rather than caution or fearfulness (vv. 2-3)?

8. Teresa wrote that physical concerns should always be subordinate to spiritual concerns. What do you find in this Scripture passage to confirm her opinion?

9. Although our spiritual journey is difficult, Teresa said that the Lord recompenses us generously for our struggles and suffering. How did this prove true in the life of Jesus (v. 2)?

10. How has this proved true in your own life? That is, how has the Lord more than made up for your spiritual struggles and difficulties?

11. Why should we willingly endure discipline from God (vv. 4-11)?

12. This passage from Hebrews concludes with encouragement (vv. 12-13). Where do you find the same sort of encouragement in the excerpt from Teresa's writing?

ALONG THE ROAD——————————————————————

❷ No matter how sincerely we resolve to keep pursuing God, fears and misgivings can continue to trouble us and hold us back. Choose one or more solid pieces of encouragement from this study (words from Scripture, Teresa's words or your own paraphrase). Write them where you will see them often. Tell them to yourself when you are discouraged, fearful or tempted to give up.

❷ Christ did not allow himself to be stopped or sidetracked in his journey to the cross. Try to imagine the results if he had quit half-way through his mission. Take time to thank him for going through with his purpose in life and giving himself for you. Write a prayer of gratitude and praise, make up a poem or song, draw a picture or express your gratitude to him in some other creative way.

❷ Make a map of your spiritual journey so far. Draw signs to identify special features such as bumpy roads, smooth stretches, detours, hazards or scenic views. As much as possible, write in dates to mark various stages of the journey. Keep the map and add to it as your journey progresses. You will probably not be able to create new parts of the map as they happen, but you will identify them as you look back.

⌔ Pack a travel trunk for your spiritual journey. Itemize the spiritual qualities you need in order to persevere and see the journey through to completion. Choose small objects to symbolize each of those qualities. Pack the objects in a container that symbolizes your travel trunk. You should pack a quality even if you don't think you possess it yet; the symbol will serve as a reminder that you and the Lord are still working on that item. Add other objects to symbolize other spiritual qualities as you realize you need them.

II
FREEDOM TO LOVE
1 Corinthians 13

*I*f you think of cats as aloof and distant creatures, you've never met our big cat, Jeeves. Jeeves loves everybody. He is aggressively friendly. He jumps into any available lap, purring and kneading with his front paws and tipping his head to one side in a charming manner.

After living with Jeeves for several years, we suspect that deep in his feline heart, he is selfish in his love. Yes, he loves, but more than that, he loves to be loved. If ignored or mistreated, he would leave us and find a new home where he was appreciated.

When we love, we want our love to be returned. It's natural. But is it necessary? Is it even helpful?

The following excerpt was written in the midst of a controversy over reforms Teresa was making in the Carmelite Order. Here's a little more background.

Its specific purpose was to serve as a guide in the practice of prayer and it sets forth her counsels and directives for the attainment of spiritual perfection through prayer. It was composed by St. Teresa at the express command of her superiors [most likely in 1565 or 1566], and was written during the late hours in order not to interfere with the day's already crowded schedule.

Through the entire work there runs the author's desire to teach a deep and lasting love of prayer beginning with a treatment of the three essentials of the prayer-filled life—fraternal love, detachment from created things, and true humility. St. Teresa's counsels on these are not only the fruit of lofty mental speculation, but of mature practical experience.*

 LEARNING TO PRAY

THE WAY OF PERFECTION

It should be noted here that, when we desire anyone's affection, we always seek it because of some interest, profit or pleasure of our own. Those who are perfect, however, have trodden all these things beneath their feet—the blessings which may come to them in this world, and its pleasures and delights—in such a way that, even if they wanted to, so to say, they could not love anything outside God, or unless it had to do with God. What profit, then, can come to them from being loved themselves?

When this truth is put to them, they laugh at the distress which had been assailing them in the past as to whether their affection was being returned or no. Of course, however pure our affection may be, it is quite natural for us to wish it to be returned. But, when we come to evaluate the return of affection, we realize that it is insubstantial, like a thing of straw, as light as air and easily carried away by the wind. For, however dearly we have been loved, what is there that remains to us? Such persons, then, except for the advantage that the affection may bring to their souls (because they realize that our nature is such that we soon tire of life without love), care nothing whether they are loved or not. Do you think that such persons will love none and delight in none save God? No; they will love others much more than they

---

*Introduction to *The Way of Perfection,* in *Complete Works of Teresa of Ávila,* trans. E. A. Peers (New York: Sheed & Ward, 1946).

did, with a more genuine love, with greater passion and with a love which brings more profit; that, in a word, is what love really is. And such souls are always much fonder of giving than of receiving, even in their relations with the Creator Himself. This, I say, merits the name of love, which name has been usurped from it by those other base affections.

Do you ask, again, by what they are attracted if they do not love things they see? They do love what they see and they are greatly attracted by what they hear; but the things which they see are everlasting. If they love anyone they immediately look right beyond the body (on which, as I say, they cannot dwell), fix their eyes on the soul and see what there is to be loved in that. If there is nothing, but they see any suggestion or inclination which shows them that, if they dig deep, they will find gold within this mine, they think nothing of the labor of digging, since they have love. There is nothing that suggests itself to them which they will not willingly do for the good of that soul since they desire their love for it to be lasting, and they know quite well that that is impossible unless the loved one has certain good qualities and a great love for God. I really mean that it is impossible, however great their obligations and even if that soul were to die for love of them and do them all the kind actions in its power; even had it all the natural graces joined in one, their wills would not have strength enough to love it nor would they remain fixed upon it. They know and have learned and experienced the worth of all this; no false dice can deceive them. They see that they are not in unison with that soul and that their love for it cannot possibly last; for, unless that soul keeps the law of God, their love will end with life—they know that unless it loves Him they will go to different places.

Those into whose souls the Lord has already infused true wisdom do not esteem this love, which lasts only on earth, at more than its true worth—if, indeed, at so much. Those who like to take pleasure in worldly things, delights, honors and riches, will account it of some worth if their friend is rich and able to afford them pastime and pleasure and recreation; but those who already hate all this will care little or nothing for such things. If they have any love for such a person, then, it will be a passion that he may love God so as to be loved by Him; for, as I say, they know that no other kind of affection but this can last, and that this kind will cost them dear, for which reason they do all they possibly can for their friend's profit; they would lose a thousand lives to bring him a small blessing. Oh, precious love, forever imitating the Captain of Love, Jesus, our Good!

 GROUP DISCUSSION OR PERSONAL REFLECTION——

1. To what extent do you agree with Teresa that "when we desire anyone's affection, we always seek it because of some interest, profit or pleasure of our own"? Why?

2. Teresa wrote that those who do not care whether their love is returned "will love others much more than they did, with a more genuine love." Why would a disregard for being loved lead to loving others more?

3. What difference does it make in our attitude toward people when we "look right beyond the body, fix our eyes on the soul and see what there is to be loved in that"?

4. Teresa said that we will find "gold" in people if we dig deep, and that we will not mind the effort of digging. When have you discovered "gold" in a person you had previously overlooked? What effort did it require on your part?

 INTO THE WORD

5. *Read 1 Corinthians 13.* How does this passage compare with what Teresa wrote about love in the excerpt above?

6. Which virtues and gifts does Paul mention as commendable but inferior to love?

7. In this passage what does Paul say about our love being returned?

8. Consider verses 4-7 in light of Teresa's words about mining for "gold" in other people. How do the difficult instructions in these verses become easier when we believe there are treasures to be found in others?

9. In verses 11-12 Paul describes the process of maturing into adulthood. How does this fit into his discourse on Christian love?

10. How can love be said to be the opposite of selfishness?

11. Paul elevated love above even faith and hope (v. 13). How would faith and hope be marred by an absence of love?

 ALONG THE ROAD————————————————————

Ask the Lord to bring to mind the names and faces of people who have seen "gold" in you and have been willing to dig for it. Thank God for each of those people. If there are some you have never thanked, and you can still get in touch, consider how you might express your gratitude for their love.

Think of someone who consistently fails to return your love. How are you affected by that person's indifference or resentment? Choose a period of time—a day, a week, maybe only an hour—and love that person as though the return of love did not matter to you. Write about any differences you notice in your own attitudes and in the relationship.

Imagine that your study group (or church, or some other Christian group in which you are involved) is going on a "gold rush" to mine for treasures in other people. Write a story, play or poem to describe what happens.

② Prospectors are sometimes tricked by "fool's gold." The substance appears genuine, but when put to the test, it proves worthless. Identify some "fool's gold" properties in people which appear valuable on the surface but have no true worth. Construct a test (a set of circumstances) which would prove whether the "gold" is real or fake.

III

RECONCILIATION AMONG BELIEVERS
Matthew 18:21-35

We don't have statistics to quote, but we suspect that many people who leave the church do so because they can't stand all the fighting that goes on. However, the issues so important to the combatants often seem trivial to people not caught up in the fight.

Teresa had shockingly strong words about the destructive power of conflict among Christians. What she had to say about the nuns in her convent also speaks to believers in any fellowship.

 THE END OF CRANKINESS

THE WAY OF PERFECTION

If one of you should be cross with another because of some hasty word, the matter must at once be put right and you must betake yourselves to earnest prayer. The same applies to the harboring of any grudge, or to party strife, or to the desire to be greatest, or to any nice point concerning your honor. (My blood seems to run cold, as I write this, at the very idea that this can ever happen, but I know it is the chief trouble in convents.) If it should happen to you, consider yourselves lost. Just reflect and realize that you have driven your Spouse from His home: He will have to go and seek another abode, since you are driving Him from His own house. Cry aloud to His Majesty and try to put things right; and if frequent confessions and communions do not mend them, you may well fear that there is some Judas among you.

For the love of God, let the prioress be most careful not to allow this to occur. She must put a stop to it from the very outset, and, if love will not suffice, she must use heavy punishments, for here we have the whole of the mischief and the remedy. If you gather that any of the nuns is making trouble, see that she is sent to some other convent and God will provide them with a dowry for her. Drive away this plague; cut off the branches as well as you can; and, if that is not sufficient, pull up the roots. If you cannot do this, shut up anyone who is guilty of such things and forbid her to leave her cell; far better this than that all the nuns should catch so incurable a plague. Oh, what a great evil is this! God deliver us from a convent into which it enters: I would rather our convent caught fire and we were all burned alive. As this is so important I think I shall say a little more about it elsewhere, so I will not write at greater length here, except to say that, provided they treat each other equally, I would rather that the nuns showed a tender and affectionate love and regard for each other, even though there is less perfection in this than in the love I have described, than that there were a single note of discord to be heard among them. May the Lord forbid this, for His own sake. Amen.

 GROUP DISCUSSION OR PERSONAL REFLECTION——

1. These instructions were written for nuns living in a convent under strict rules and authority. At what points do Teresa's words

still apply to Christians everywhere?

2. Teresa wrote that though her blood runs cold at the thought of grudges, party strife and desire to be greatest among the nuns. She termed this discord "the chief trouble in convents." In your own experience, where have you known the same sort of conflict to be "the chief trouble" among Christians?

3. Teresa makes the extreme statement that rather than have conflict among the nuns, she "would rather our convent caught fire and we were all burned alive"! What makes strife among believers so terrible?

4. Christians have always disagreed over matters of style, conscience and doctrine. How would you explain the difference

between such disagreements and the type of discord Teresa so
greatly feared?

 INTO THE WORD

5. *Read Matthew 18:21-35.* Scan verses 15-20 for Jesus' words
leading up to this passage. What prompted Jesus to tell this parable
(vv. 21-22)?

6. When Peter asked his question in verse 21, what answer do
you think he hoped to receive?

7. How did Jesus' answer go beyond anything Peter or the other
disciples might have expected?

8. Identify how you personally respond to Jesus' answer to Peter.

9. When have you received the type of forgiveness Jesus mandates here?

10. In the parable, how did the master respond to the servant's plea, and with what results (vv. 23-27)?

11. By contrast, how did the servant respond to his fellow servant's plea (vv. 28-30)?

12. The servant's lack of mercy altered the relationship between him and his master (vv. 31-34). How did the master now choose to deal with the servant and why?

13. Consistent forgiveness would have changed the outcome of Jesus' parable. When have you seen forgiveness change the outcome of a situation?

14. Verses 34 and 35 are harsh, though perhaps no harsher than Teresa's statement that "I would rather our convent caught fire and we were all burned alive." With such a strong warning coming directly from Jesus, why do you think Christians resist reconciliation and hold onto grudges?

 ALONG THE ROAD————————————————————

Consider a time you were reconciled with another believer. Draw a staircase or a path to show the steps that led to reconciliation. Identify any points where the process got stalled or side-tracked, and note how you got unstuck.

⊘ In a journal entry, write about what keeps you going forward toward reconciliation when you are at odds with another believer. First write about the specifics of particular situations. Then make more general statements about what motivates you to keep moving toward reconciliation.

⊘ Picture yourself as the forgiven servant in Jesus' parable. Imagine your emotions as you face the master, beg for mercy and are forgiven. Picture yourself leaving the king's presence and meeting a fellow servant who owes you something—perhaps money, more likely something else (such as consideration, time, an admission of error or a confession of guilt). Whose face do you see on your fellow servant? What does he or she owe you? What will it take for you to respond with mercy? Make specific plans to show mercy to your fellow servant. Your response may be purely internal or may require outward action.

IV

WHAT ABOUT MY RIGHTS?

1 Peter 2:18-25

*I*t's not fair! A neighbor keeps taking a shortcut across our backyard on his motorcycle. The person at the next desk assaults us daily with her sickly sweet cologne. A family member spills a secret that gets twisted in the telling and retelling. Unfair, we say. Unfair! Unfair!

Teresa of Ávila would agree that we all experience the unfairness of life. She would also remind us that we are in good company. If Jesus is our Lord, we must remember that he was the victim of the ultimate injustice. Why should our experience be any different from his?

Jesus did more than suffer injustice passively. He responded in genuine strength. By considering his response, we learn what to do when our rights are stepped on or denied.

 WHAT ABOUT JESUS' RIGHTS? ———————

THE WAY OF PERFECTION

I often tell you, sisters, and now I want it to be set down in writing, not to forget that we in this house, and for that matter anyone who would be perfect, must flee a thousand leagues from such phrases as: "I had right on my side;" "They had no right to do this to me;" "The person who treated me like this was not right." God deliver us from such a false idea of right as that! Do you think that it was right for our good Jesus to have to suffer so many insults, and that those who heaped them on Him were right, and that they had any right to do Him those wrongs? I do not know why anyone is in a convent who is willing to bear only the crosses that she has a perfect right to expect: such a person should return to the world, though even there such rights will not be safeguarded. Do you think you can ever possibly have to bear so much that you ought not to have to bear any more? How does right enter into the matter at all? I really do not know.

Before we begin talking about not having our rights, let us wait until we receive some honor or gratification, or are treated kindly, for it is certainly not right that we should have anything in this life like that. When, on the other hand, some offense is done to us (and we do not feel it an offense to us that it should be so described), I do not see what we can find to complain of. Either we are the brides of this great King or we are not. If we are, what wife is there with a sense of honor who does not accept her share in any dishonor done to her spouse, even though she may do so against her will? Each partner, in fact, shares in the honor and dishonor of the other. To desire to share in the kingdom of our Spouse Jesus Christ, and to enjoy it, and yet not to be willing to have any part in His dishonors and trials, is ridiculous.

 GROUP DISCUSSION OR PERSONAL REFLECTION——

1. What is the "false idea of right" from which Teresa begs God to deliver her and the sisters?

2. Under what circumstances have you made complaints like the ones that Teresa quotes in the first sentence of this excerpt?

3. How do Teresa's words challenge contemporary views of life?

4. How do her words challenge your view of life?

 INTO THE WORD ————————————————————

5. *Read 1 Peter 2:18-25.* Although this passage begins with an appeal to slaves (v. 18), it quickly becomes generalized to all Christians. What is the main point Peter is making? Try to express it in one sentence.

6. Common sense tells us that people should suffer for doing bad and be rewarded for doing good. How does Peter turn that idea on its head (vv. 19-20)?

7. Peter wrote, "To this you were called" (v. 21). How do you interpret "this"?

8. In what ways did Jesus suffer unjustly? Refer to the 1 Peter passage and your own knowledge of the Gospels.

9. How did Jesus respond to unfair attacks against himself (vv. 22-24)?

10. We can't bear other people's sins on a cross or heal others by our wounds (v. 24); only Christ can do that. But what are some ways we can still imitate Jesus' response to unfairness?

11. When we suffer injustice, what difference does it make to know that God is "the one who judges justly" (v. 23)?

12. What connection do you see between returning to Christ our Shepherd and Overseer (v. 25) and handling injustice in a Christ-like manner?

 ALONG THE ROAD————————————————————

Teresa wrote, "Let us wait until we receive some honor or gratification, or are treated kindly, for it is certainly not right that we should have anything in this life like that." This week, every time you receive a compliment or experience some blessing, try to challenge yourself with this question: "Do I really deserve this, or is it an unmerited kindness from God and from others?" The aim is not self-abasement or false modesty; the aim is freedom from the demand to be honored.

◯ Think about people and circumstances currently stepping on your rights. Prayerfully consider one way you will respond to them this week as Christ would respond.

◯ First Peter 2:21 says, "To this you were called, because Christ suffered for you, leaving you an example, that you should follow in his steps." Compile a list of ways Jesus was dishonored. Draw a small footprint beside each one which you feel you have also suffered to some extent.

First Peter 4:13 says, "But rejoice that you participate in the sufferings of Christ, so that you may be overjoyed when his glory is revealed." Thank God for the privilege of sharing in Christ's sufferings. For further encouragement, read Philippians 1:29, Romans 8:17 and Romans 5:3-5.

V

MORE LIKE CHRIST
2 *Corinthians 12:1-10*

*H*ow do we evaluate Christian ministries? Often we use the same standard of success used by the world. This television ministry has a budget of so many million; that church has grown by X percent; this evangelist preaches to so many hundreds of thousands per year.

What about an urban storefront ministry barely scraping by, a pastor struggling with private temptations or a church youth program losing ground against sports and television? They wouldn't want to be sized up by their failures and weaknesses. They certainly wouldn't brag about them!

Then how could the apostle Paul dare to say, "I will boast of the things that show my weakness" (2 Corinthians 11:30)? Like Paul, Teresa found that struggles and setbacks become blessings as they shape our character to be more like Christ.

 ENDURING DIFFICULTIES ————————————

INTERIOR CASTLE: SEVENTH MANSIONS

It will be a good thing, sisters, if I tell you why it is that the Lord

grants so many favors in this world. Although you will have learned
this from the effects they produce, if you have observed them, I will
speak about it further here, so that none of you shall think that He
does it simply to give these souls pleasure. That would be to make a
great error. For His Majesty can do nothing greater for us than grant
us a life which is an imitation of that lived by His Beloved Son. I feel
certain, therefore, that these favors are given us to strengthen our
weakness, as I have sometimes said here, so that we may be able to
imitate Him in His great sufferings.

We always find that those who walked closest to Christ Our Lord
were those who had to bear the greatest trials. Consider the trials
suffered by His glorious Mother and by the glorious Apostles. How
do you suppose Saint Paul could endure such terrible trials? We can
see in his life the effects of genuine visions and of contemplation
coming from Our Lord and not from human imagination or from
the deceit of the devil. Do you imagine that he shut himself up with
his visions so as to enjoy those Divine favors and pursue no other
occupation? You know very well that, so far as we can learn, he
took not a day's rest, nor can he have rested by night, since it was
then that he had to earn his living. I am very fond of the story of
how, when Saint Peter was fleeing from prison, Our Lord appeared
to him and told him to go back to Rome and be crucified.*

We never recite the Office on his festival, in which this story is
found, without my deriving a special consolation from it. How did
Saint Peter feel after receiving this favor from the Lord? And what
did he do? He went straight to his death; and the Lord showed him
no small mercy in providing someone to kill him.

Oh, my sisters, how little one should think about resting, and
how little one should care about honors, and how far one ought to
be from wishing to be esteemed in the very least if the Lord makes

---

*"In the old Carmelite Breviary, which St. Teresa would have used, the Antiphon of
the Magnificat at First Vespers on June 29 runs: 'The Blessed Apostle Peter saw
Christ coming to meet him. Adoring Him, he said: "Lord, whither goest Thou?" "I
am going to Rome to be crucified afresh." ' The story has it that St. Peter returned
to Rome and was crucified." Footnote to *Interior Castle,* in *Complete Works of Teresa of Ávila,* trans. E. A. Peers (New York: Sheed & Ward, 1946).

His special abode in the soul. For if the soul is much with Him, as it is right it should be, it will very seldom think of itself; its whole thought will be concentrated upon finding ways to please Him and upon showing Him how it loves Him. This, my daughters, is the aim of prayer: this is the purpose of the Spiritual Marriage, of which are born good works and good works alone.

 GROUP DISCUSSION OR PERSONAL REFLECTION——

1. According to Teresa, why does God grant us "so many favors in this world," and what is a mistaken reason for believing he grants those favors?

2. How do you respond to the statement "We always find that those who walked closest to Christ Our Lord were those who had to bear the greatest trials"?

3. Teresa wrote that the aim of prayer is to find ways to please the Lord and show him how much we love him. How do her reasons for prayer compare with the usual reasons most of us pray?

INTO THE WORD

4. *Read 2 Corinthians 12:1-10.* Some of the Christians in Corinth were challenging Paul's authority as an apostle of Christ. In this letter he defended himself and his ministry. Rather than throw his weight around, Paul said he preferred to come as a servant in the spirit of Christ. He admitted his own shortcomings yet strongly asserted his authority as an apostle.

Many believe that the man in verses 2-4 is Paul himself, especially since in verse 7 he says he was in danger of conceit "because of these surpassing great revelations." What had this "man in Christ" experienced (vv. 1-4)?

5. In the face of such privilege from God, why did Paul continue to emphasize his own weaknesses (vv. 5-6)?

6. It is easy to see how a person could brag about strengths. How could a person brag about failings?

7. Why did Paul refrain from boasting (v. 6)?

8. Paul hoped the Lord would answer his prayers by removing a "thorn," whatever it was. How does the Lord's answer surpass even the removal of the problem (vv. 9-10)?

9. What new insight did Paul gain about the purpose of weakness in a Christian's life (vv. 9-10)?

10. When have you prayed like Paul for some affliction to be removed, and it has remained?

11. How have you come to see Christ's grace to be enough for your needs or his power showing itself through your weakness, as he promised in verse 9?

 ALONG THE ROAD

What is the greatest thing God could do for you? Consider Teresa's words "His Majesty can do nothing greater for us than grant us a life which is an imitation of that lived by His Beloved Son." How does your desire fit with developing a life that is more Christlike?

Jesus is saying the words of 2 Corinthians 12:9 directly to you. Write Jesus' promise on several 3 x 5 cards, as many as you need, and place them where you will see them in situations where you are weak: spiritually, emotionally, morally, even physically. If you prefer, add Paul's statement from verse 10, "When I am weak, then I am strong."

Write out your thoughts about a particular "thorn" you bear which God has not taken away. Write honest prayers about it.

Reflect on any good that has come from the thorn in your life and in the lives of others.

✑ Construct a play in which the apostle Paul comes for a job interview to be a pastor or missionary. During the interview, Paul consistently downplays his strengths and highlights his own weaknesses and the power of Christ within him. How do you think the interviewer(s) would react? What would they say? Would Paul get the job?

VI

GOD'S INFINITE GOODNESS

Psalm 138

When we fall in love with someone, that person becomes our favorite topic of conversation. We'll talk about our beloved with anybody who will listen and even with those who would rather not. We describe our special person's likes and dislikes, outstanding qualities, talents, sense of humor and latest profound remark. But talking about the beloved is not enough. We need to talk with that special person in intimate conversation.

A big part of Christian fellowship is talking with each other about our Lord. We're encouraged when we remind each other of the Lord's faithfulness. We're stimulated when we discuss theology and learn to respect each other's differences. But our spiritual lives eventually go dry if we only talk *about* the Lord. We must also talk *with* him in sincere prayer.

Teresa had written a draft of her spiritual autobiography, *The Life of Teresa of Jesus,* in 1562. Within a few months she was commanded by her superiors to write an expanded account of her life. She completed this second version in 1565, about the time she began work on *The Way of Perfection.*

This excerpt from Teresa's writing is different from the other quotes that have appeared in this study. While the others are addressed to the nuns under her care, here she turns to her Lord and addresses him directly in a lavish outburst of praise. We can sense that Teresa turned to God with such praise in her heart countless times not recorded on paper.

 WORSHIPING GOD———————————————————

LIFE OF TERESA

O infinite goodness of my God! It is thus that I seem to see both myself and Thee. O Joy of the angels, how I long, when I think of this, to be wholly consumed in love for Thee! How true it is that Thou dost bear with those who cannot bear Thee to be with them! Oh, how good a Friend art Thou, my Lord! How Thou dost comfort us and suffer us and wait until our nature becomes more like Thine and meanwhile dost bear with it as it is! Thou dost remember the times when we love Thee, my Lord, and, when for a moment we repent, Thou dost forget how we have offended Thee. I have seen this clearly in my own life, and I cannot conceive, my Creator, why the whole world does not strive to draw near to Thee in this intimate friendship. Those of us who are wicked, and whose nature is not like Thine, ought to draw near to Thee so that Thou mayest make them good. They should allow Thee to be with them for at least two hours each day, even though they may not be with Thee, but are perplexed, as I was, with a thousand worldly cares and thoughts. In exchange for the effort which it costs them to desire to be in such good company (for Thou knowest, Lord, that at first this is as much as they can do and sometimes they can do no more at all) Thou dost prevent the devils from assaulting them so that each day they are able to do them less harm, and Thou givest them strength to conquer. Yea, Life of all lives, Thou slayest none of those that put their trust in Thee and desire Thee for their Friend; rather dost Thou sustain their bodily life with greater health and give life to their souls.

GROUP DISCUSSION OR PERSONAL REFLECTION——

1. How do you interpret Teresa's statement "Thou dost bear with those who cannot bear Thee to be with them"?

2. Teresa wondered why "the whole world" does not strive to draw near to God. What are some reasons people avoid God?

3. This prayer includes the interesting statement that ungodly people "should allow Thee to be with them for at least two hours each day, even though they may not be with Thee." How would this advice help a person who is on the fence spiritually, seeking God but avoiding him at the same time? How would you advise a seeking person to put this suggestion into practice?

4. Even believers may have trouble concentrating on the Lord for one hour a week during a church service. What are some practical ways we can allow the Lord to "be with us for at least two hours each day"?

 INTO THE WORD ───────────────────────────

5. *Read Psalm 138.* How does the psalmist demonstrate that he, like Teresa, is "wholly consumed" in love for the Lord?

6. What words and phrases does the writer use to show that God is above everything and everyone else (vv. 1, 2, 4, 5)?

7. How had the Lord blessed this writer?

8. Teresa said that concentrating on the Lord takes effort. What effort did the psalmist put forth (vv. 1-3)?

9. How does God show his concern for people in need (vv. 3, 6-8)?

10. Why do you think God would have a different relationship with "the lowly" than with "the proud" (v. 6)?

11. What confidence did the psalmist express in verse 8?

12. In what sense do you share the psalmist's confidence, and

how would you like to share it more deeply?

 ALONG THE ROAD————————————————————————

🕿 We all seek God for many reasons, but Teresa emphasized one reason in particular: "Those of us who are wicked, and whose nature is not like Thine, ought to draw near to Thee so that Thou mayest make them good." As your relationship with God has deepened, how has your character changed? (Others who know you well may be able to answer more objectively than you can.)

🕿 Schedule a block of time to simply allow the Lord to "be with you," and for you to be with him. Plan to go somewhere as quiet as possible. Take along your Bible, a songbook or any other helps which will focus your mind and heart on Christ. Perhaps you will want to go out into nature with a sketching pad or notebook and allow God to speak to you through natural surroundings. Maybe you will choose to sit in a crowded mall and watch people, who are made in the image of God. Don't be surprised if your attention wanders from God, even in a quiet spot with your Bible in front of you. When that happens, pray about whatever has distracted you. Don't

worry if your time turns out to be longer or shorter than you origi-
nally planned. Make plans to set aside another block of time soon.

🖉 Freely express your own praise to the Lord, using whatever
medium is natural for you: writing, speaking aloud, singing, draw-
ing, making something or doing whatever expresses the Lord's "infinite goodness."

How to Lead a Christian Classics Bible Study

If you are leading a small group discussion using this series, we have good news for you: you do not need to be an expert on Christian history. We have provided the information you need about the historical background in the introduction to each study. Reading more of the original work of these writers will be helpful but is not necessary. We have set each reading in context within the introductions to each study. Further background and helps are found in the study notes to each session as well. And a bibliography is provided at the end of each guide.

In leading the Bible study portion of each study you will be helped by a resource like *Leading Bible Discussions* in our LifeGuide® Bible Study series as well as books dealing with small group dynamics like *The Big Book on Small Groups*. But, once again, you do not need to be an expert on the Bible. The Bible studies are designed to follow the flow of the passage from observation to interpretation to application. You may feel that the studies lead themselves! The study notes at the back will help you through the tough spots.

What Is Your Job as a Leader?

☐ To pray that God will be at work in your heart and mind as well as in the hearts and minds of the group members.

☐ To thoroughly read all of the studies, Scripture texts and all of the helps in this guide before the study.

☐ To help people to feel comfortable as they arrive and to encourage everyone to participate in the discussion.

☐ To encourage group members to apply what they are learning in the study session and by using the "Along the Road" sections between sessions.

Study Notes

Study One. Get Moving! Hebrews 12:1-13.
Purpose: To spur us toward bold perseverance in our spiritual travels.
Question 2. Without humility, we will compare our spiritual progress with that of other people and congratulate ourselves on how well we're doing (or how well we imagine we're doing!). Teresa even said that we should regard others as advancing faster than we are. Notice also that she said we will be miserable living this way unless we practice self-renunciation.
Question 4. Love turns us outward to others. If we are busy seeking consolations from God, our attention will be on ourselves and how much or how little we are being comforted.
Question 8. Teresa's statement is revolutionary in a culture that elevates physical beauty, long life and athletic achievement. She did not write that the body does not matter at all, only that it is far less important than the spirit. Anxiety over physical health does not help the spirit and may even be detrimental to the body.

Jesus, our example, willingly endured physical suffering and death to give us eternal life (v. 2). Earthly discipline almost always involves physical constraint or discomfort, which we endure for the sake of our character (vv. 7-11). Teresa herself was plagued with persistent illness, but she refused to let physical weakness defeat her spiritual purpose.
Question 9. For example, Jesus could endure the cross because he was mindful of the coming joy in heaven at his Father's right hand.

Study Two. Freedom to Love. 1 Corinthians 13.

Purpose: To encourage us in unselfish love in imitation of Christ.

Question 6. The gift of speaking in tongues (vv. 1, 8); prophecy (vv. 2, 8); knowledge (vv. 2, 8); faith (vv. 2, 13); giving away all we possess (v. 3); martyrdom (v. 3); hope (v. 13). Without love, these gifts and actions may be used for selfish and prideful purposes or may degenerate into mere show. Love turns these other qualities outward where they are used by God to serve others.

Question 7. Paul had nothing to say in this passage about our love being returned. His emphasis was completely on loving, not being loved.

Question 9. Apparently Paul regarded a Christian as still immature if that Christian is elevating any other spiritual quality above love. Other spiritual gifts, no matter how attractive, are imperfect and will disappear "when perfection comes" (v. 10).

Question 11. Outstanding faith can lead us to plunge ahead fearlessly into new ministries, but without love, we will run over other people in our zeal. Outstanding hope makes us confident of our own future, but without love we will care little for what happens to other people.

Study Three. Reconciliation Among Believers. Matthew 18:21-35.

Purpose: To lead us to give up destructive conflict and reconcile with believers.

Question 5. Although the parable was immediately prompted by Peter's question about forgiveness, Jesus had been talking about how to deal with a fellow Christian who sins against us (vv. 15-17).

Question 6. Peter may have been hoping to sound generous in his forgiveness. Surely forgiving seven times would be going beyond the call of duty! Or perhaps Peter was looking for an upper limit: beyond seven times, he would not have to forgive.

Question 7. Jesus' answer has been read as "seventy-seven times" or "seventy times seven." In either case, seven is the biblical number of perfection. It can be taken as "an infinite number of times."

Study Four. What About My Rights? 1 Peter 2:18-25.

Purpose: To find joy in our participation in the sufferings of Christ.

Question 3. Contemporary thought puts great emphasis on demanding our individual rights and the rights of our class or group. We may ask, what's wrong with that? Shouldn't Christians defend and even fight for the rights of others? And what about our own rights to practice our faith? Those are legitimate questions. The distinction drawn in the study note for question 10 may be helpful.

Question 6. Peter indicates that it is better for a person to suffer for doing right than for doing wrong! Notice, however, the condition in verse 19: the person endures unjust suffering "because he is conscious of God."

Question 9. Verse 22 quotes Isaiah 53:9. Isaiah 53 is the "Suffering Servant" chapter that prophesied that the Messiah (Christ) would be rejected, mocked and killed. Isaiah 53 makes it clear that the Messiah suffered according to the will of God. Christ submitted to death in order to offer himself for humanity's sin. He was able to resist the temptation to defend himself only because he surrendered fully to the will of God and trusted God for his vindication.

Question 10. A distinction should be made between demanding our own rights and standing up for the rights of others. Jesus stood up for people who were mistreated or belittled by those more powerful. He paid special attention to people who had the least power and status in his society: lepers, widows, beggars and small children. God's concern for justice is a strong theme running throughout the entire Bible. Neither the apostle Peter nor Teresa tells us to ignore the rights of others. They only urge us to leave our own rights in the hands of God "who judges justly" (1 Pet 2:23).

Question 12. Verse 12 contradicts the idea that giving up one's rights is a sign of weakness. If Christ is Shepherd and Overseer, then he is strong enough to lead and govern the world. His willing surrender of himself is not a mark of weakness but of strength.

Study Five. More Like Christ. 2 Corinthians 12:1-10.

Purpose: To acknowledge our weaknesses and rely on Christ for strength.

Question 3. Often we pray in order to find solutions for our own problems and to make life more bearable for ourselves. Certainly God does invite us to bring all our concerns to him (for example, Ps 62:8; Heb 4:16; 1 Pet 5:7). However, Jesus said that the most important commandment given by God is to "love the Lord your God with all your heart and with all your soul and with all your mind and with all your strength" (Mk 12:30). Our ultimate aim should be loving God, with all other aims subordinate to that one. Then, like Paul with his thorn in the flesh, we will find that chronic problems actually draw us to love and trust God more deeply.

Question 4. Paul "has felt forced by the apparent claims of his opponents in Corinth to visions to refer to his own visionary experiences. Rather than roll out a list of his experiences, starting with the Damascus road incident [Acts 9], he cites the one vision that he knows will top any of theirs, a vision in which his experience of heaven was so real that he is not sure if it was a vision or a physical rapture to heaven" (Walter C. Kaiser Jr. et al., eds., *Hard Sayings of the Bible* [Downers Grove, Ill.: InterVarsity Press, 1996], p. 626).

Question 7. There have been centuries of speculation over the nature of Paul's "thorn in the flesh." Suggestions include physical illness, temptations and opposition to the gospel. "There are some things that we can definitely say about the 'thorn.' First, it was evil. It is described as a 'messenger of Satan,' not as an angel of God. This means that it comes from the Evil One with evil intent. . . . Second, God was allowing this thing. This is what appears to be indicated by 'there was given me.' . . . Third, the 'thorn' caused some type of weakness. . . . In this weakness Paul knew that God's strength could be shown" (*Hard Sayings,* pp. 627-28). Remarkably, Paul prayed for the removal of his thorn only three times (v. 8). Most of us would probably pray for relief that many times a day! Perhaps the identity of Paul's thorn is left vague so all believers can find a connection with him as we go to the Lord with our problems, express our feelings honestly and then leave the outcome with him.

Questions 8-9. Grace, God's undeserved favor, was offered to Paul at exactly the same time he was receiving undeserved pain. The two coexisted within him. The grace of Christ was sufficient for Paul; yet grace did not wipe out his pain. Christ had a purpose for Paul that was greater than the relief of suffering. This purpose could be accomplished only if Paul's thorn remained with him. Christ's power would be "made perfect" in Paul's weakness. "Perfect" here can mean "complete" or "mature." Paul came to understand and even to embrace the Lord's purpose, even though it required him to suffer. He took joy in knowing that because of his weakness, the power of Christ would show even more strongly in his life.

Study Six. God's Infinite Goodness. Psalm 138.

Purpose: To continually be drawn to God as the object of our love.

Question 2. Our natural first response is to look critically at the lives of worldly people. We should also search our own hearts concerning times we try to evade God, perhaps by staying overly busy or avoiding prayer and worship.

Question 5. Note especially verses 1 and 2, although the entire psalm is an expression of deep devotion.

Question 6. The psalmist will sing the praise of the one true God before other "gods" (v. 1); God's name and word are above all other things (v. 2); all the kings of the earth should praise God (vv. 4-5). The term "gods" in verse 1 may refer to false gods, the idols that people set up on earth; or it may refer to human judges, who are called to judge according to God's will and always subordinate to God's judgment.

Question 7. The writer mentions the Lord's help in the past (v. 3), the present (v. 7) and the future (v. 8). He does not reveal the specifics of his problems or the Lord's help. As with Paul's unidentified "thorn" in Study 5, we can put our own experiences into this psalm and praise God along with the writer.

Question 9. This God who is above everything and everyone still takes care of "the lowly," and, in fact, he is closer to them than to "the proud" (v. 6).

Sources

Study One
Interior Castle: Third Mansions 2.

Study Two
The Way of Perfection 6.

Study Three
The Way of Perfection 7.

Study Four
The Way of Perfection 13.

Study Five
Interior Castle: Seventh Mansions 4.

Study Six
Life of Teresa 8.

Further Reading

Donze, Mary Terese. *Teresa of Ávila*. New York: Paulist, 1982.

Hamilton, Elizabeth. *Saint Teresa: A Journey to Spain*. New York: Charles Scribner's, 1959.

Hatzfeld, Helmut A. *Santa Teresa de Ávila*. New York: Twayne, 1969.

Nevin, Winifred. *Teresa of Ávila: The Woman*. Milwaukee: Bruce, 1956.

Walsh, William Thomas. *Saint Teresa of Ávila: A Biography*. Milwaukee: Bruce, 1943.

Teresa of Ávila. *The Way of Perfection*.

———. *The Collected Works of St. Teresa of Ávila*. Translated by Otilio Rodriguez. ICS Publications, 1976.